First Family

By Deborah Hopkinson   Illustrated by AG Ford

KATHERINE TEGEN BOOKS
An Imprint of HarperCollins Publishers

For my own family, and for

families (and first dogs) everywhere

—D.H.

To my loving mother and father

—A.F.

Katherine Tegen Books is an imprint of HarperCollins Publishers.

First Family

Text copyright © 2010 by Deborah Hopkinson

Illustrations copyright © 2010 by AG Ford

www.harpercollinschildrens.com

Library of Congress Cataloging-in-Publication Data

Hopkinson, Deborah.

First family / by Deborah Hopkinson ; illustrated by A.G. Ford. — 1st ed.

p.   cm.

ISBN 978-0-06-189680-4 (trade bdg.)

1. Obama, Barack—Family—Juvenile literature.   2. Presidents—United States—Family—Juvenile literature.

I. Ford, A. G., ill.   II. Title.

E909.O22.H675   2010   973.932092—dc22   2009024450   CIP   AC

Typography by Rachel Zegar

10 11 12 13 14   CG/WOR   10 9 8 7 6 5 4 3 2 1

❖

First Edition

INAUGURATION DAY!

As Barack Obama stepped forward to take the oath of office as America's forty-fourth president, he placed his hand on the Lincoln Bible, held by his wife, Michelle, the new First Lady. Their daughters looked on with proud, sunny smiles.

Americans gained more than a new leader on January 20, 2009. They opened their hearts and welcomed a new First Family.

That same afternoon, the White House halls hummed with activity as people bustled to move in the new First Family.

The White House staff hung clothes in the right closets, stacked books on shelves, and planned a scavenger hunt to help Malia and Sasha learn their way around the 132 rooms of the grand historic mansion.

That night the Obama family slept for the first time in their private quarters, a special part of the main White House residence on the second floor.

Marian Robinson, Michelle's mom and the First Grandmother, moved into a guest room on the third floor, where she'd be close enough to help out and be part of her granddaughters' lives every day.

The new First Family was home.

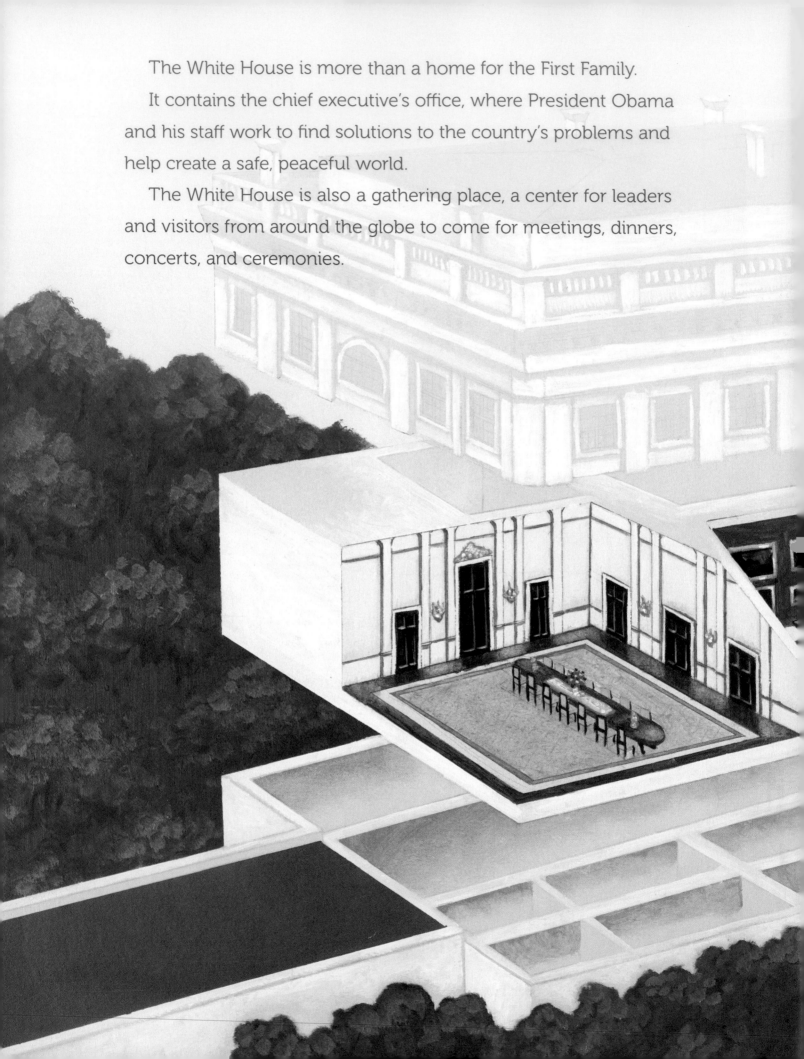

The White House is more than a home for the First Family.

It contains the chief executive's office, where President Obama and his staff work to find solutions to the country's problems and help create a safe, peaceful world.

The White House is also a gathering place, a center for leaders and visitors from around the globe to come for meetings, dinners, concerts, and ceremonies.

And the White House is a museum. Some rooms are open to the public for part of the day so people can visit treasures of America's past—paintings, delicate china, antique clocks and furniture. Children and families come from all over to stand where history has been made—and continues to be made. That's why the White House is called the People's House.

The White House belongs to us all.

"Beep! Beep! Beep!" Time to wake up! A day in the White House begins early.

Malia and Sasha set their own alarms so they won't be late for school. The girls also make their beds and straighten up their rooms. They do chores every day, because Mom and Dad still make the rules. Malia and Sasha each have their own bedrooms, which they're allowed to decorate however they want.

The First Family pays for its own food, although there are chefs and others on staff to order supplies and cook meals. Nearly a hundred people—carpenters, chefs, butlers, and housekeepers—work to take care of the White House and make the First Family comfortable.

The president and First Lady are two of the busiest people in the world. But they're not too busy to exercise. President Obama wakes up early to work out in the White House gym six days a week. Michelle spends time on the treadmill. She also lifts weights and jumps rope.

The White House grounds are a wonderful place for an early morning walk. The First Family has a big yard—the Obamas live on about eighteen acres of grass and gardens called the President's Park. Bo can't wait to go outside each morning. How he loves to run!

Every weekday, Malia and Sasha head out to school. Usually their grandma goes with them to drop them off and give them a good-bye hug.

To make sure they're safe, agents of the United States Secret Service drive them in special cars. In fact, the Secret Service protects the Obamas whenever they leave their private quarters in the White House.

"Rosebud and Radiance are ready for school!"

To help keep track of the First Family, each person is given a special code name, or nickname. (The names aren't secret, but they do help the agents do their jobs more easily.)

President Obama's name is Renegade, the First Lady is known as Renaissance, Malia is Radiance, and Sasha is Rosebud.

And if Bo gets a code name, it will probably be Rascal.

When it's time for work, the president doesn't have far to go. President Obama can simply walk downstairs to the Oval Office, on the first floor of the West Wing.

Each president can choose furnishings from the White House collection. President Obama decided to keep the Resolute desk, which was made of oak from a British ship, the HMS *Resolute*, in 1880. Many presidents, including John F. Kennedy, Bill Clinton, and George W. Bush, have chosen to use this historic desk.

First Lady Michelle Obama has an office on the opposite side of the White House, in the East Wing.

When the girls are off to school, the First Lady begins her busy day.

Michelle Obama has devoted her career to community service, and being the First Lady allows her to continue doing what she loves. Sometimes she visits schools to read to children. She speaks to young people, telling them about her own dreams and how she worked hard for an education. With her winning smile, ready laugh, and big hugs, Michelle has warmth, glamour, and charm.

Wherever she goes, at home or around the world, America's First Lady inspires people to work together for what they believe.

The First Lady also serves as the White House hostess. That means working with White House chefs to plan menus for events and state dinners, and perhaps even designing a new set of china. Michelle chose huckleberry cobbler as the dessert for her first state dinner. That's a First Family favorite.

For President Obama, each day brings new challenges and responsibilities. The president's decisions and policies can change the lives of millions of people.

When he's not working in the Oval Office, the president travels to other parts of the United States to learn about problems there. He also visits other countries to meet with world leaders. Part of his job is working together with other nations on issues affecting everyone, like combating climate change, keeping the world safe, and having clean air and water for all.

President Obama's airplane is Air Force One. The president often rides to and from the air base in a helicopter, Marine One. If he's been away, Malia and Sasha know their dad's on the way home when they hear the helicopter overhead.

Sometimes the First Family travels together to spend the weekend back in Chicago, where they used to live, or at Camp David, a private retreat in the Maryland countryside for the president.

Helicopters are exciting, but they're noisy too.

As he reads, writes, or talks on the phone at his desk in the Oval Office, President Obama can look out on the Rose Garden, where many ceremonies and press conferences are held.

He can also wave at the girls when they get back from school—especially if they're playing on their swing set. Malia and Sasha's "castle" is a fun addition to the White House yard.

Afternoons are also a good time to check on the White House Kitchen Garden, which Michelle planted with the White House chefs and fifth graders from a local school. The garden is on the South Lawn. The First Family grows more than fifty kinds of vegetables, including lettuces, broccoli, snap peas, onions, and spinach.

Eating fruits and vegetables is important to the First Family. Michelle wants every family to think about healthy eating. Weeding a garden is good exercise too. Even the president takes his turn.

One of the most popular members of the First Family is Bo, the First Dog.

On election night, Barack Obama told the whole country that he'd promised Malia and Sasha a puppy. After months of waiting, Bo, a six-month-old Portuguese water dog, finally arrived. Bo was a present from Senator Edward M. Kennedy. No one was happier than Sasha and Malia, who could wrap their arms around the newest member of the First Family at last.

On rainy days, Malia and Sasha explore the amazing place where they live. They can look at the wonderful American paintings in the Green Room or stand in the Blue Room, where President Abraham Lincoln signed the Emancipation Proclamation.

They can visit the State Dining Room, with its long table and shiny mirrored centerpiece. It's elegant now, but when Theodore Roosevelt was president he hung a moose head over the mantel.

The White House even has its own bowling alley and a movie theater. Best of all, the White House has secret passageways. One leads to a tunnel underneath the White House to the Treasury Building. There's also a hidden door in the Queen's Bedroom on the second floor. Inside is a staircase that leads upstairs to the Solarium, with beautiful views of the sky and Washington, DC.

There's no doubt about it: The White House is a great place for hide-and-seek.

If there are no evening events to attend, the First Family eats dinner together.

Malia and Sasha help set the table and bring out the food. It's rewarding to eat a salad made with lettuce from your own garden.

This is the best time to talk about the good parts and the hard parts of everyone's day. The Obama family calls this daily sharing "the roses and the thorns."

The president has many problems to solve. It's no wonder his daughters understand that being the chief executive of an entire nation can sometimes be a "thorny job."

After dinner it's time to read and study or finish up that last bit of homework.

Malia once told her dad she wanted to study in the Lincoln Bedroom, at the same desk that President Abraham Lincoln once used.

That would certainly help her think big thoughts.

After one last walk, Bo is ready for bed. So are Sasha and Malia.
The best nights are when their parents are home to read aloud,
give good-night hugs, and tuck them in.

Every First Family since John Adams, the second president, has lived in the White House. Although being in the First Family brings many duties and responsibilities, it's also a privilege.

For the Obamas, it's clear that just being together every day with the ones they love is the best part of all.

WHITE HOUSE FACTS AND FIRST FAMILY TRIVIA

★ On Inauguration Day 2009, the Capitol was draped with five large flags: a fifty-star flag in the center, flanked by two twenty-one-star flags representing the president's home state of Illinois, the twenty-first state in the Union, with two thirteen-star flags on each side.

★ The tradition of the First Family moving into the White House on Inauguration Day began with President William Henry Harrison and his family in 1841.

★ President Woodrow Wilson's luggage was misplaced on his inauguration day, so he spent his first night as president without his pajamas.

★ Inauguration Day has been January 20 since 1937.

★ By the middle of the twentieth century, the custom of moving the new First Family in at noon on January 20 had begun.

★ The White House has 132 rooms—including 35 bathrooms!

★ The White House has its own bowling alley, movie theater, tennis court, putting green for golf, and even an outside swimming pool.

★ At first, the White House was lit by candles and oil lamps. In 1848 the White House got gas lighting and then electricity in 1891.

★ The Resolute desk was given to President Rutherford B. Hayes by Queen Victoria in 1880. It is made of wood from the HMS *Resolute*, a British ship that was abandoned after it became stuck in Arctic ice in 1854 but later broke free and was towed to harbor by an American ship.

★ The United States Secret Service has been providing security for presidents since 1901 and for all members of the First Family since 1917. The Secret Service does not go into the family's private quarters.

★ It's a custom that the code names of each member of the First Family start with the same letter.

✶ The White House Kitchen Garden, begun on the South Lawn in 2009, is the first vegetable garden at the White House since 1943.

✶ First Families have kept many pets. Alice Roosevelt, the daughter of President Theodore Roosevelt, had a green snake named Emily Spinach.

✶ President Coolidge and his family kept many pets at the White House, including canaries, a raccoon named Rebecca, and ducklings that the First Lady kept in the bathtub until they got so big she gave them to the National Zoo.

✶ The Kennedy children, Caroline and John Jr., had a pony named Macaroni.

✶ Portuguese water dogs trace their history back to ancient times when these working dogs helped fishermen off the coast of Portugal. The first Portuguese water dogs came to the United States in 1968.

For more fun facts and to learn more about the White House,
visit the official White House website:

http://www.whitehouse.gov/about/white_house_101/